PIANO | VOCAL | GUITAR

MAROON 5
IT WON'T BE SOON BEFORE LONG!

ISBN 13: 978-1-4234-3349-1
ISBN 10: 1-4234-3349-1

HAL•LEONARD®
CORPORATION
7777 W. BLUEMOUND RD. P.O. BOX 13819 MILWAUKEE, WI 53213

Visit Hal Leonard Online at
www.halleonard.com

IF I NEVER SEE YOUR FACE AGAIN

Words and Music by ADAM LEVINE
and JAMES VALENTINE

*Recorded a half step higher.

MAKES ME WONDER

Words by ADAM LEVINE
Music by ADAM LEVINE,
JESSE CARMICHAEL and MICKEY MADDEN

Moderately fast

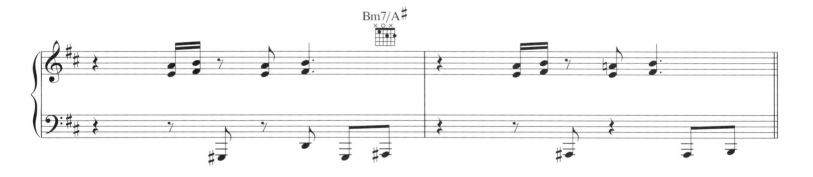

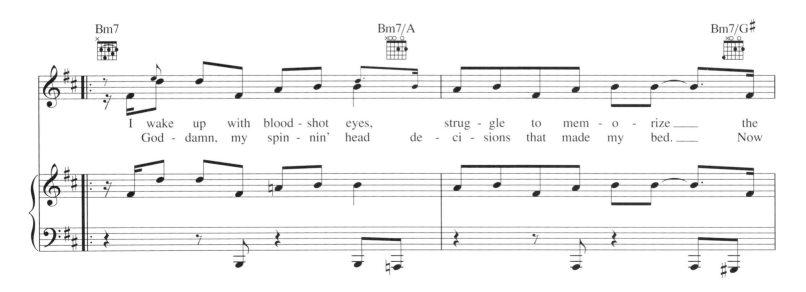

I wake up with blood-shot eyes, strug-gle to mem-o-rize ____ the
God - damn, my spin-nin' head de - ci - sions that made my bed. ____ Now

One day I'll wake up and it won't hurt an-y-more.

You caught me in a lie;

I have no al-i-bi. The words you say don't have a

mean-ing, ___ 'cause I still don't have ___ the rea-

LITTLE OF YOUR TIME

Words and Music by
ADAM LEVINE

Please don't leave, stay in bed, touch my bod-y in-stead, __ gon-na make you feel it, __

__ can you still feel it? Gon-na make you feel it, __ can you still feel it?

Oh, __ my, I don't mind be-ing the oth-er guy, nice try for these

WAKE UP CALL

Words and Music by ADAM LEVINE
and JAMES VALENTINE

Moderate groove

I did-n't hear what you __ were say - ing, I live on raw e - mo - tion, ba - by.

I an-swer ques-tions nev - er, may - be. And I'm not kind if you __ be-tray me,

so who the hell are you __ to say we nev-er would have made __ it, babe. __ If you need-

WON'T GO HOME WITHOUT YOU

Words and Music by
ADAM LEVINE

NOTHING LASTS FOREVER

Words and Music by
ADAM LEVINE

Moderate Rock

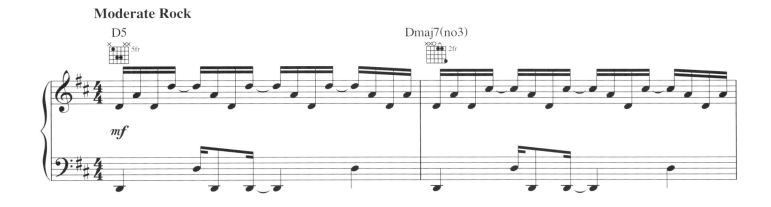

It is so ___ eas-y to see ___ dys-func-tion be-tween you ___ and me, ___ we must ___
bed that's warm ___ with mem-o-ries ___ can heal ___ us tem-po-rar-i-ly, ___ but mis-

CAN'T STOP

Words and Music by ADAM LEVINE
and JAMES VALENTINE

All a - lone ___ in my room, ___ think of you ___ at a rate ___
Can't be - lieve ___ I could think ___ that ___ she ___ would just fol -

___ that is tru - ly a - larm - ing.
- low me ev - 'ry - where I go.

GOODNIGHT GOODNIGHT

Words and Music by
ADAM LEVINE

NOT FALLING APART

Words and Music by
ADAM LEVINE

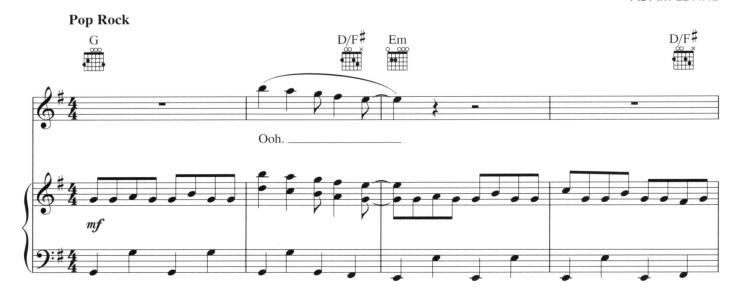

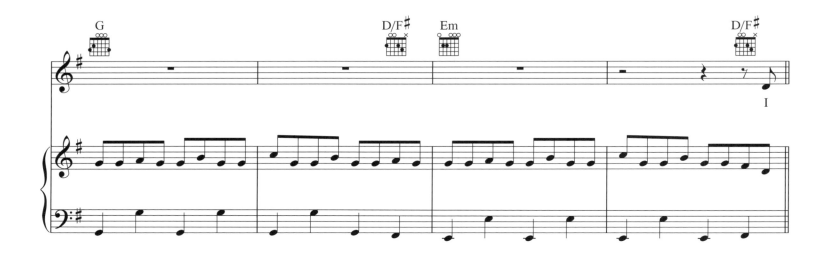

50

KIWI

Words and Music by ADAM LEVINE
and JESSE CARMICHAEL

Funk Rock

You're such a flirt, I know you hurt and so do I, I

em-pa-thize. I see you out, you nev-er cared, a con-ver-sa-tion we nev-er shared.

But it's so strange, it's

some-thing new, a - maz - ing feel-ings that I have for you.

I close my eyes when I'm a - lone, won-der what it be like to

make you moan. I want to give you some-thing bet - ter than

an - y - thing you've ev - er had, a strong-er and a fast - er lov - er.

stop it be - fore it be - gins.

Guitar solo

BETTER THAT WE BREAK

Words and Music by
ADAM LEVINE

Moderate Ballad

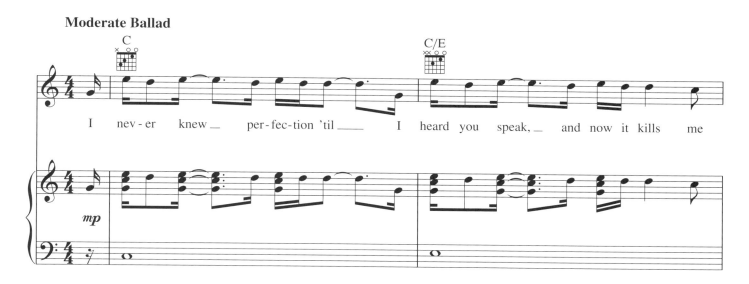

I nev-er knew ___ per-fec-tion 'til ___ I heard you speak, ___ and now it kills me

just to hear you ___ say ___ the sim-ple things. ___ Now

break-ing up ___ is hard ___ to do, sleep-ing's im-pos-si-ble too, ___ and

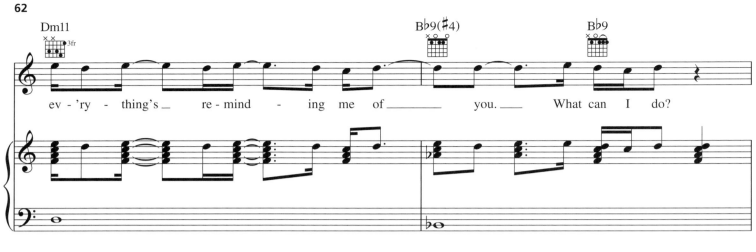

ev - 'ry - thing's __ re - mind - ing me of _____ you. ___ What can I do?

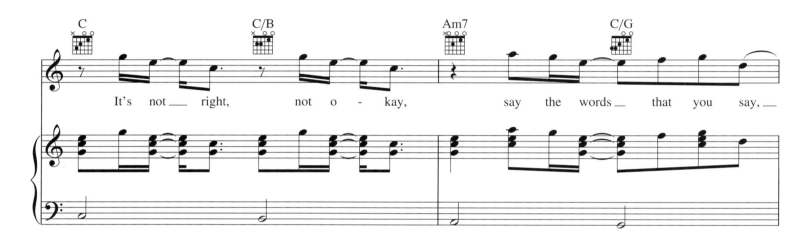

It's not __ right, not o - kay, say the words __ that you say, __

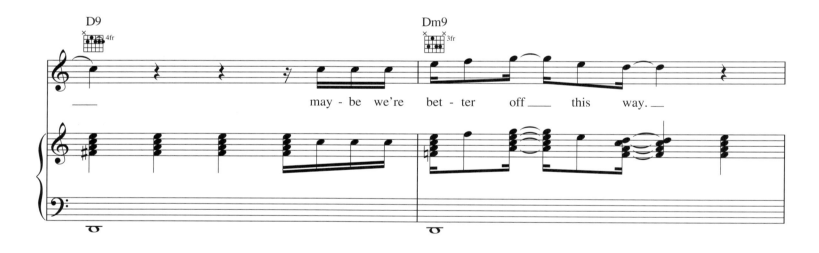

__ may - be we're bet - ter off __ this way. __

I'm not __ fine, I'm in __ pain, it's hard-er ev - e - ry day, __

64

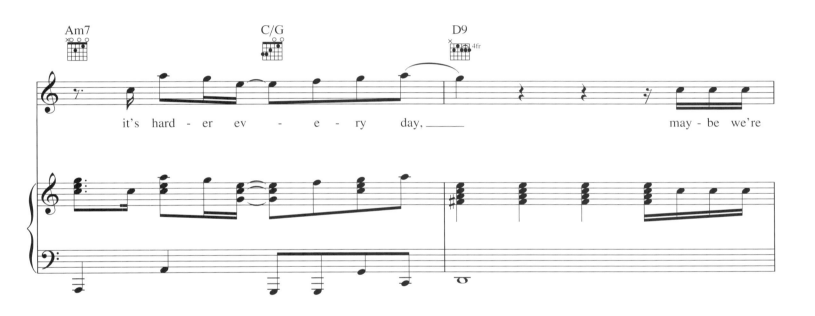

BACK AT YOUR DOOR

Words and Music by ADAM LEVINE
and JESSE CARMICHAEL